Rhymes & Damn Lies

Rhymes & Damn Lies

poetry by Mike Puhallo
cartoons by Wendy Liddle

hancock house

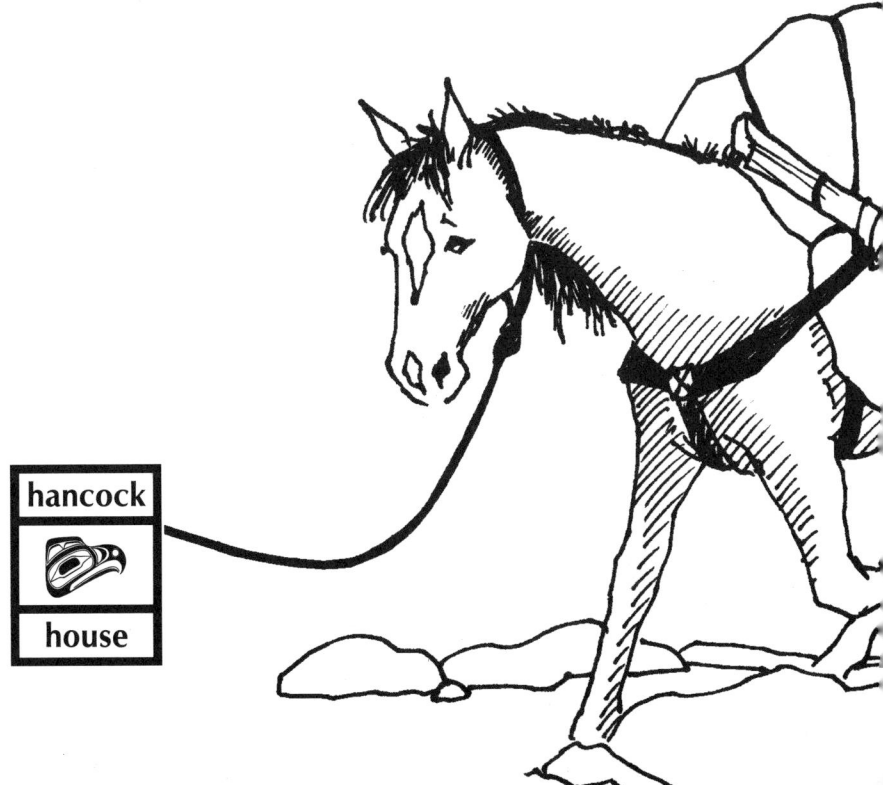

ISBN 0-88839-624-4
EAN 9780888396242
Copyright © 2006 Mike Puhallo, Wendy Liddle

Cataloging in Publication Data

Puhallo, Mike, 1953–
    Rhymes & damn lies / Mike Puhallo ; cartoons by Wendy Liddle.

    Poems.
    ISBN 0-88839-624-4

    1. Cowboys—Poetry. 2. Ranch life—Poetry. I. Liddle, Wendy
II. Title. III. Title: Rhymes and damn lies.

PS8581.U42R48 2006   C811'.54   C2006-900342-4

All rights reserved. No part of this publication may be reproduced, stored in a retrieval system or transmitted, in any form or by any means, electronic, mechanical, photocopying, recording, or otherwise, without the prior written permission of Hancock House Publishers.
Printed in Indonesia—TK PRINTING

Editor: Theresa Laviolette
Production: Laura Michaels
Cover Design: Ingrid Luters
Cover Illustration: Wendy Liddle

We acknowledge the financial support of the Government of Canada through the Book Publishing Industry Development Program (BPIDP) for our publishing activities.

Published simultaneously in Canada and the United States by

HANCOCK HOUSE PUBLISHERS LTD.
19313 Zero Avenue, Surrey, B.C. Canada V3S 9R9
(604) 538-1114 Fax (604) 538-2262

HANCOCK HOUSE PUBLISHERS
1431 Harrison Avenue, Blaine, WA U.S.A. 98230-5005
(604) 538-1114 Fax (604) 538-2262

Website: **www.hancockhouse.com**
Email: **sales@hancockhouse.com**

Contents

Cowboy Gatherings	7
The Fine Art of Hurling Defecation	8
Headin' into Town!	10
Forty Below	11
The Tender Trap	12
Scour Pills and Roses	13
Springtime on the Ranch	14
Ma's New Pocket-Size Cow Dog	16
I Owe You, Bob!	17
The Guy on the Radio Says It's Spring!	18
Easter 2003	19
Road Kill (Again!)	20
Jump Start Your Day	22
As Good As It Gets	25
A Scene That's Best Unseen	26
Just Passin' Thru	27
Drifters	28
Bob Jesson	29
Dog Creek, Where Our Traditions Began	30
Fifty's Just a Number!	31

The Dream Team of the Cariboo 32
500 Years in the Saddle 34
Chee Witt 36
Bulls Don't Care 37
Doc Mason 38
Little White Lies 40
If He Could Read My Mind ? 41
Kenny McLean 42
Adios Ken 44
Elko 45
Fuzzy Politics 46
Dear George, Maybe We Can Help Next Time .. 47
Lest We Forget 48
The Strenuous Life? 49
The Gathering 50
Winter Across the Rockies 51
Cow Country Christmas Memory 52
The Christmas Tree Hunt 53
Adios Aught–3! 55
Just Keep Dancin'!!! 56
Courage 57
To All the Volunteers 58
Tales of the Cariboo Trail 59
Royal Memories 60
Like Wow Man! 62
Weaning Time 63

Cowboy Gatherings

Relax old friend, and sit a spell,
we'll swap some yarns and lies.
Sing cowboy songs,
and tell some poems
about bad broncs and circle flies.

We'll listen to the old tunes,
and some that are brand new,
along with rhymes and stories,
from a cowboy's point of view.

For the story of the West ain't done;
there are pages yet to turn.
Where cattle graze and horses run,
and flickering campfires burn.

The silver screen has lost its luster;
the paperback hero has faded away.
And the working cowboy of the real west
is finally having his say!

The Fine Art of Hurling Defecation
(Composed While Cleaning the Barn)

It's one of those chores a fellow keeps putting off,
but it lies in wait for you,
until you run out of reasons to procrastinate,
or just got nothing better to do.

So you gather fork and shovel,
the front-end loader just won't fit.
The barns and pens need cleaning,
because you're about knee deep in ...it.

Fertilizer for the pasture,
that's where I spread this defecation.
And in agriculture as in literature,
...it requires careful application.

Ask any poet, scribe, or farmer,
they all understand the trick.
On the page or in the pasture,
just don't lay it on too thick!

Headin' into Town!

I don't know why it always snows the most,
on the days I plan to go to town.
But with a little weight in the back and studded tires,
I can always get around.

I have no fear of snowy roads,
whiteouts or icy curves.
It's dodging all them city folk,
that really tests my nerves.

Death and taxes are plumb certain,
all weathermen are liars.
And towns are full of lunatics,
skating around on summer tires.

Forty Below

The hard-packed snow creaks,
beneath the tractor wheels,
in the half-light before dawn.
Lined cover-alls, felt pack boots,
and your "Elmer Fudd" hat on.

Still you curse the cold that numbs your face,
and makes the frost on your moustache grow.
You kind of wish it would warm up a bit,
but that would just bring more snow.

Fahrenheit or Celsius
The only thing for sure you know:
When the diesel gels and your truck won't start,
forty below is… forty below!

The Tender Trap

It's been said that good intentions,
can cause a lot of grief.
We're up against a stacked deck, boys,
at least that's my belief.

Diamonds are for rich folks,
and chocolate makes her fat.
Valentine's Day has become a trap,
there is no denying that!

Red roses may be the safest bet,
to show your Darlin' that you care.
But supply and demand comes into play,
when those posies get quite rare!

The lady in the flower shop
takes your cash, and smiles real nice.
You could have bought them flowers
a week ago
for about one tenth
the price.

Scour Pills and Roses

Well! So it is, once again,
that romantic time of year.
Time to tally up the vet supplies,
'cause calving time is near.

Sulpha drugs and penicillin,
Scour pills and a dozen roses.
Rubber gloves and Vaseline,
to rub on frostbit noses.

At least two dozen needles,
some iodine and suture string.
I make a list of the stuff we need
to get us through 'til spring.

So I gas up the pick-up,
off to town before everything closes,
for groceries and essential stuff,
like scour pills and a dozen roses.

Spring Time on The Ranch

(My Annual Ode to Mud)

"Use the back door! Scrape your boots!
Don't track that mud in here!"
I retreat real quick, head 'round the back,
while mumbling, "Yes dear."

It's calving time; we're in and out,
three dozen times a day,
She really ain't got a hope in heck,
of keeping that mud at bay.

The commandments never vary,
resistance would cause strife.
She must have learned it from my mother,
'cause I've heard it all my life!

It's the ranch wife's ritual springtime chant,
for six weeks every year.
"Use the back door! Scrape your boots!
Don't track that mud in here!"

Ma's New Pocket-Size Cow Dog

My wife got herself a new puppy
that ain't more than six inches tall.
Hannah, the Min-Pin, is a cute little rascal,
but as dogs go, she is awful small.

Border collies are the only kind of dogs,
that I have ever chosen to own.
And I've sure never had no use for lap dogs,
if the simple truth be known.

But Ma still has her job in town,
to help keep the bank at bay.
So I have this tiny canine companion,
with me on the farm all day.

To the barn cats and the cattle,
she shows no trace of fear,
although she hides in my coat pocket,
when my horses come too near.

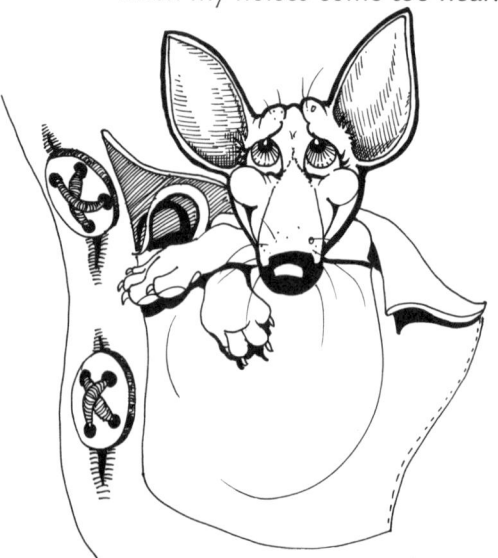

I Owe You, Bob!

"For a promise made is a debt unpaid"...
Bob Service penned that phrase,
in the morbid tale of Sam McGee,
back in the Gold Rush days.
Now Bob worked in the banking trade,
which was respectable back then.
But he had a passion for the rowdy tales
of lost and restless men.

The muck and mire of mine and creek,
the card shark and faded dove,
were but the powder and the lipstick,
on Bob's true "Light O' Love !"

"A promise made is a debt unpaid!"
A sacred pact between Bob and I,
to preserve the folklore of our beloved West
and never let the stories die!

The Guy on the Radio Says It's Spring!

The snow in the valley is prit' near gone,
there's some green on the southern slope.
Spring is a time of muddy boots,
new life and renewed hope.

The horses fed, I pause by the barn,
feeling much at ease,
as I drink the sounds and smells,
that ride the gentle southern breeze.

A subtle sound seems out of place.
I soon locate the source
of the drip and gurgle of running water:
a broken line in the stock tank of course.

My joyful bliss on this sweet spring morn,
has turned into a bummer.
I trade my cowboy hat for a baseball cap.
Today I am the plumber!

Easter 2003

Ancient wounds begin to bleed,
when we take up our guns
and seek to right a wrong by laying low
some other mothers' sons.

Now, I ain't no saint or prophet,
my faith is far too weak.
And I know some will shout in anger
at the simple words I speak.

Yet I know with all my being,
when nations go to war,
he that came to show the way,
is on the cross once more!

As I said I am no preacher,
but the words rang clear and true,
All I could do is write 'em down,
and pass them on to you.

Road Kill (Again!)

Well I found out why Billy Gates

called his new operating system **"X-P"**

because my hard drive just **X-P**loded!

The head techno-nerd said he'd never heard

or seen a wreck like that,

except maybe when his pick-up fan

chewed up the neighbor's cat!

He done his best to save my files,

and extract them all with care,

but the bits and bytes began to fight...

and there was muffins everywhere!

Next week sometime they'll have it fixed,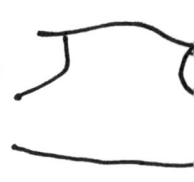

so I'll put the muffins in the mail,

and spend the next few days moving cows,

where there ain't no cyber trail!

Jump Start Your Day

You know for a middle aged ex bull rider,
my little brother still runs pretty good.
We jumped the horses in the trailer,
and as I tied my mare in place,
my little brother stood at the back door,
a late starter in this race.
At least it was a gentle grade...
I hollered, "Run! Gordy! Run!"
when the truck and trailer started moving,
'cause the brake had come undone.
I couldn't do a thing from where I was,
so I hung on for the ride.
The rig had a pretty good head start
before ol' Gordy hit his stride.
But like I said the grade was gentle,
so he stopped that run-away.
And there's nothing like a little excitement,
to begin a cowboy's day.
I suppose some day we'll get that E-brake fixed,
but now it's time to hit the road,
out looking for stray cattle
...and a flat place to unload.

As Good As It Gets

My little brother just finished his first trip
as an assistant guide.
Leading a party of American hunters
on a big game hunt far and wide.

He said he had to do all cooking,
and carry most of the gear,
While the hunters and the head guide
searched for moose and deer.

But he claimed it was a lot more fun
than hunting with me and dad.
Because this time he was getting paid,
to do the same chores he always had!

A Scene That's Best Unseen

A true tale. One thing about folks out in the Chilcotin: they are about as western as you can get without fallin' in the ocean!

The story of Big Creek's "peerless lady wing-shot"
is sure to draw a smile,
as she relaxes in her bubble bath,
in fine Chilcotin style.
She demurely draws her daily bath,
then calmly loads her gun,
then settles in the tub, out on the lawn,
to soak up suds and sun!
For sport she picks off swallows,
and she don't miss, Ol' Pard.
So, God help any stranger,
who should wander in the yard.
This story is the blessed truth,
no word of lie I speak,
But her heart is pure, and her aim sure,
an' it would cost your life to peek!

Just Passin' Thru

I rode the river trail today,
on the sorrel,
two-year old.
She's still a little cold backed,
but she steps out nice and bold.
It's an easy half-day circle,
no cows to move today,
It's mild for late November,
the sky's a dull slate gray.
A good day
to ride a young horse,
along a winding river trail.
one horse one man,
no sense of time,
no tests,
to pass,
or fail.

Drifters

A cowboy songwriter friend, from Louisiana,
stopped to visit for at time.
We swapped some lies and points of view,
on music craft and rhyme.

He'd been on the road for several months,
playing little halls and coffee bars,
One of them modern day drifters,
cowboys with guitars.

We sip coffee in the kitchen
and watch two bears cross my back yard.
He remarks them was the first bears that he'd seen this trip,
and he'd been looking pretty hard.

Them bears are looking for windfall apples,
that singing cowboy is in search of a song.
They stare at each other through a thin pane of glass.
Soon each will be moving along.

Bob Jesson

1914 – August 8, 2003

A tall man on a bay horse,
That's the picture in my head.
"Best all around horseman I ever met,"
was what my father said.

From the Gang Ranch to Spruce Meadows,
to the green pastures at Noble Creek,
when true horsemen come together,
it's of men like Bob they speak.

From riding rough string in the thirties,
to show ring of today,
in a lifetime spent on horseback
he explored a better way.

These days it's all big-money boys,
every trainer's holding clinics.
They've got videotapes and "how to" books,
marketing plans, and gimmicks.

They will teach you all their secrets
for five hundred bucks a lesson.
But I grew up watching horsemen,
like Lalonde, McDonnell, and Jesson.

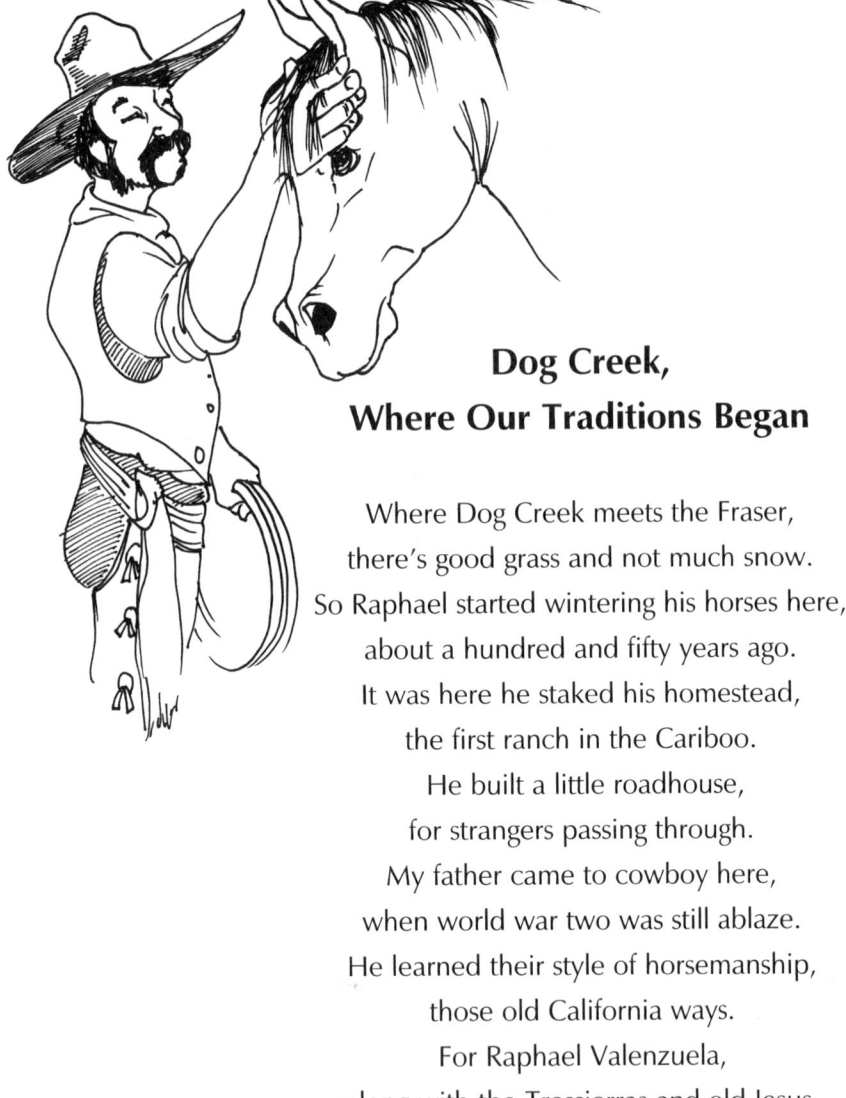

Dog Creek, Where Our Traditions Began

Where Dog Creek meets the Fraser,
there's good grass and not much snow.
So Raphael started wintering his horses here,
about a hundred and fifty years ago.
It was here he staked his homestead,
the first ranch in the Cariboo.
He built a little roadhouse,
for strangers passing through.
My father came to cowboy here,
when world war two was still ablaze.
He learned their style of horsemanship,
those old California ways.
For Raphael Valenzuela,
along with the Tressierras and old Jesus,
left their mark on the style and methods,
that most BC horsemen use!

The English came with money,
the Scots might know a cow.
But, when it came to handling horses,
those old vaqueros taught us how!

Fifty's Just a Number!

Riding along the river trail,
a soft April rain is falling.
Above its subtle whisper,
I hear wary, wild geese calling.

I close my eyes and drift a while,
to hoof beats on soft ground.
The damp earth smell,
the sounds of spring,
envelop and surround.

Time really has no meaning,
it hasn't changed the things that count.
The sounds and smells of April,
a gentle rain, and a willing mount.

The Dream Team of the Cariboo

Way back in the nineteen thirties,
they where mighty hard to beat.
The hockey team from Alkali Lake,
who would not accept defeat.

You know there wasn't very many of them,
so they could not often change their line.
The other teams had about twenty guys,
Alkali just nine.

Mathew Dick, he was the goalie,
Clemine and Johnson played defense.
Sylista was their center,
and man he was intense.

Pat Chelsea and Alfred Sandy,
were Sylista's two main wingers.
Joe Dan, Gaby Jack, and Squinahan
where back up, the second stringers.

They went by team and wagon,
gone at least three days for every game.
No matter who they played that year,
it ended up the same.

In ragged wore out uniforms,
and old skates with buckskin laced.
They where the champions of the Cariboo
and beat every team they faced!

They even went down the coast,
and played against the best,
and lost that series by just one goal,
against the All Stars of the West!

Just nine young Indian cowboys,
who came from Alkali.
But boy, they could play hockey,
put on them skates and fly.

The New York Rangers tried to hire Sylista,
but their deal he wouldn't take.
He said "You know, I already got a job,
I cowboy for Alkali Lake."

In honor of David Johnson, Mathew Dick, Alec Antoine (Sylista), Joe Clemine, Pat Chelsea, Joe Dan, Alfred Sandy, Gaby Jack, and Francis Squinahan, and also Louie Amiel and Peter Christopher from Canim Lake who joined them for the Vancouver series.

Some of this hockey team's members were also very well known for their exploits in the rodeo arena.

Alec Antoine (Sylista) was struck by lightning while fixing a fence in 1938; he died a few months later. Without him the team never again reached the same level of competition. Lester Patrick was the New York Rangers Scout who offered Sylista an NHL contract.

500 Years in the Saddle

The last cattle drive of the millennium
it seems hard to grasp somehow.
Five hundred years since those Spanish ships
arrived with the first horse and cow.

Those vaqueros from the deserts of Sonora,
Way down in old Mexico,
crossed the rugged Sierra with their cattle,
about three centuries ago.

On those California ranchos and missions
cows and horses sure multiplied,
under the care of those spade-bit horsemen
who taught the whole West how to ride.

They drove herds clean up into Oregon
Shaniko and Willamette Valley way.
and sold them to the Kin-Chutchmen
who worked for the old Hudson's Bay.

When the gold rush raged in the rivers and creeks
from Yale to Barkerville,
cattle came north by the thousands
those hungry bellies to fill.

There were Scots who'd given up on the fur trade,
And a pair of Virginians there too,
with the Metis and California vaqueros
who would have made up that first drover crew.

As we ride on the trails that they followed,
and gaze at the landmarks they saw,
we honor those who blazed these trails,
when this land was still wild and raw.

Over a century and a half since those first cattle drives,
but the spirit of the West still lives on.
and riders have gathered from near and far,
to saddle their ponies at dawn.

Yes, folks still toil with horses and cattle,
living the life we love best.
New friends and old, still sharing the dream,
of cowboyin' out in the West.

Chee Witt

Chee Witt is the Chilcotin name for chickadee. She wandered the Chilcotin Plateau most of her life, living off the land, refusing to stay indoors. They say in her youth she was an incredibly beautiful woman who was severely beaten by her jealous husband. She wandered alone for nearly half century, first with a small herd of cattle and horses, later with only what she could carry. Like the little bird she was named for she endured whatever nature threw at her, sleeping in the snow, moving where she pleased. The woman passed on more than thirty years ago but the mountain chickadee still calls to her in the spring.

In late winter Chee Witt suddenly changes her tune from the familiar "chick – de – de – de" to three long clear notes, rising then falling: "deee – deee – deeee."

Well we've got January nearly whipped,
and it's almost Groundhog Day!
With millions of folks staring into holes
just begging to be led astray.

Ah! Them rodents are all liars,
it's easy enough to see.
That's why I get my winter weather tips,
from the mountain chickadee.

When Chee Witt sings her Chinook song,
just three notes, clear and strong,
the warm days will out number the cold ones,
and winter won't last too long.

Some don't believe in legends,
but her voice was plain to me
Today I heard the springtime song,
of the mountain chickadee.

Bulls Don't Care

Well, nearly all the cows are home,
but half our bulls are still out there.
Hanging up on the summer range,
because bulls don't really care.

They'll hole up in some willow patch,
where they've got water and good grass.
Their summer work is done; they soak up the sun,
and let the autumn days slip past.

They're heedless of the winter storms,
or the fact that wolves hunt there.
We play hide and seek for half the fall,
because bulls don't really care.

Doc Mason

The twists and turns in a cowboy's life
can't hardly be anticipated.
Doc Mason was my travelling pard,
before he got educated.
Bareback horses was his specialty,
while I preferred the saddle broncs,
'though some claim we never rodeo'd half as hard,
as we worked the honky-tonks!

It took a while, but my ol' pard,
got his degree and become a vet.
While I went to raisin' cows and writin' rhymes,
and really still ain't growed up yet.

Educated and respectable,
Doc Mason's done quite well.
And there's little sign left,
of his rowdy youth,
as far as most folks could tell.

But his sense of humor hasn't changed,
although he has toned it down a mite.
And after all those years of travelling broke,
he's still... a little tight.
So when a client had a pot-bellied pig,
he wanted to have put down,
The wheels in my ol' pardner's head
started spinning 'round and 'round.

He could nearly taste the sausage,
and smell that fresh cured bacon.
Then the client mentioned the funeral plans
his wife and kids was makin'.
My ol' pardner isn't easily spooked,
but it made his client sort of nervous,
When ol' Doc asked with grave concern
if they planned an
open casket service.

Little White Lies

*After 38 years of starting colts I suspect I don't bounce as well as I did,
but I've gotten way better at avoiding the need to.*

He was five years old and still unbroke,
the owner said,
"He's been handled once or twice,
been out on pasture much since he was three,
but…his mother was real nice."
Well the big colt took the bit real well,
just a little nervous and head shy.
He barely flinched when I put the saddle on,
an' I begin to smell a lie.
So I let him stand in the round corral,
while I got the owner on the phone,
and after dancing 'round a little bit,
she confirmed what I should have known.
"Well, I had hired a kid to break him,
who lives just down the road.
But he must have
mistreated my Pretty Boy,
and that's why he
got throwed!"

Now I've been
starting colts
since I was 12,
and I've seen my
share of dirt.
Range colts and
broncs are no big
deal, but them little lies can get
you hurt!

If He Could Read My Mind?

Will Rogers once said something about horses being the only critter on earth that seemed to be designed with man in mind!

I rode the big sorrel colt again this morning,
A week into training and we ain't had a wreck.
Another three weeks he'll be gentle enough,
and I figure I will have earned my check.
You know it's been a dozen years,
since I started a colt any older than three,
so this big five year old has been a bit of a test,
and a challenge of sorts for me.
One step at a time, building knowledge and trust,
he learns to respond to the bit and each cue.
Unraveling five years of bad habits,
and figuring out what I want him to do.

Yes the horse trainer takes all the credit,
failures are blamed on the pupil of course.
Fact is, the only true key to horse training,
is the versatile mind of the horse.

Kenny McLean
1939 – 2002

On July 13, 2002 Kenny Mclean passed away. He was considered by many to be the greatest Canadian rodeo cowboy of all time and a true national hero. He was competing in a senior professional rodeo at Taber, Alberta when he suffered a fatal heart attack. He was 63 years old.

Ken was born May 13, 1939 at Okanagan Falls, BC. He was a tremendously gifted athlete who could have excelled in nearly any sport. Ken was breaking colts for his father on the ranch by the time he was twelve. By the time he was 17 he was on the road, competing in the saddle bronc riding against the best rodeo cowboys in the world, and winning.

He earned one of his first championship buckles at Kamloops rodeo in 1956. He went on to win almost every major rodeo in North America at one time or another in his career, including the Calgary Stampede.

In 1959, at the age of twenty, Kenny Mclean won his first Canadian championship in the saddle bronc riding. He won again in 1960 and 1961, becoming the first cowboy ever to be crowned Canadian Champion Bronc Rider three years in a row.

In 1961 Ken was named rookie of the year on the Rodeo Cowboys Association circuit south of the border. In 1962 Kenny McLean earned the title of World Champion Saddle Bronc Rider.

After winning a world championship riding bucking horses, Ken also began competing in the calf roping and steer wrestling. He quickly established himself as one of the best all-around cowboys in the world, winning Canadian championships in both steer wrestling and calf roping.

He was All Around Champion Cowboy Of Canada four times. Kenny Mclean still holds the record for the most major championships ever won by a Canadian cowboy (14).

Kenny McLean became the first rodeo cowboy to be inducted into the BC Sports Hall of Fame in 1974.

In 1976 he received the Order of Canada.

He is also a member of The Canadian Professional Rodeo Hall of Fame, and was inducted into the BC Cowboys Hall of Fame in July of 2001.

Kenny McLean was far more than a great athlete, he was a teacher and mentor to several generations of young Canadians both inside and outside the rodeo arena. He pioneered the concept of rodeo schools, and was so respected as a teacher that even other professional cowboys at the top of their game went to him for training. (Larry Mahan had won two world all around championships in a row when he took time off competing to attend one of Kenny's schools to sharpen his skills.)

Ken's gift as a teacher extended to horses too, and over the years he acquired a reputation as top breeder and trainer of performance horses.

He also had a subtle sense of humor and an intense competitive drive. As his wife Paula once remarked to a friend "You don't want to play Scrabble with him, he's got the whole dictionary memorized."

Kenny Mclean was the kind of role model that often seems

missing in today's society. He had a keen interest in the history and heritage of the West.

In 2001, forty-five years after he won his first silver buckle, Kenny Mclean won yet another world championship. At sixty-two years of age he won the World Senior Professional Calf Roping Championship.

When Kenny Mclean, heard the Master's call he was well mounted and he had his rope in his hand — a champion to the end.

Adios Ken

Today the West seems a little less western,
a great Cowboy's been called home.
A hint of sadness hangs in the air,
wherever good cowboys roam.
For this man was the best of the best,
in the arena or in the hills.
A salty hand in all that he did,
a master of those old vaquero skills.
And it's still the dream of every young twister,
who lives by spur and rein,
just once to hear somebody say,
"He rides like Kenny McLean."

Elko

In the deserts of Nevada,
there's a quiet old cow town,
that was on the verge of folding up,
when the nearby mines shut down.

Where Garcias made their silver bits,
and they still grazed a cow or two,
until the Government decided the wild horses,
should have all the grass that grew.

That's when Elko nearly blew away,
with nothing left to hold things down.
Rusty rails and empty store fronts,
 another soon-to-be ghost town.

Then twenty years ago some poets
gathered here to swap some lies,
and Elko started drawing crowds,
like "you know what" draws flies.

Now the place is booming,
'though the mines are still
shut down.
It's where cowboy poets
walk like kings
because their BS
saved the town!

Fuzzy Politics

Will Rogers once said,
"I don't make jokes, I just watch the government,
and report the facts."

Sorting fact from fiction,
where politics is involved,
would drive a sober man to drink,
and still get nothing solved.

They must carry on the traditions,
set in bygone days,
when our forefathers laid out their plans,
in an alcoholic haze.

Men like Amor de Cosmos, Ullyseus Grant,
and don't forget "Sir John".
Their fuzzy logic laid the foundation,
our great nations are built upon.

If we learn from the lessons of the past,
the future gets less risky.
What politics suffers from today is
too many issues, not enough whiskey!

Dear George, Maybe We Can Help Next Time...

To George Dumb-A Ooops! I mean Dubya Bush.
From Prime Minister Jean Poutine,
Commander in Chief of the Canadian Army,
Navy, and Vintage Flying Club.

We wish you good luck in your war,
as you stand upon the brink,
of your big chance to prove your manhood,
where your poppa chose to blink!

We were on our way to help you,
with everything that would fly or float,
but our ol' helicopter fell out of the sky,
and kind of busted up our boat.

And if you need help for a ground attack,
I'm afraid we just can't be the ones,
because the army clerk in Petawawa,
forgot to register our guns.

Lest We Forget

When we pause to honor the sacrifice,
of those who gave their lives and more,
let us not forget that few of them,
would have chosen to go to war.

For every life that's cast away,
leaves a family ripped and torn,
bitter tears and empty dreams,
a generation left unborn.

It is not for honor or for glory,
that a young man fights and dies.
Let us not forget their sacrifice,
Nor cheapen it with lies.

Sometimes tyrants must be stopped
and there may be no other way.
But we owe it to their memory
to keep searching for the day

when young soldiers will not have to die,
and all nations will be free,
when our leaders wage the final war
between greed and poverty.

The Strenuous Life?

The round corral is a sheet of ice,
it seems winter ain't quite gone.
I've got two fillies in to start their training,
but the crusty snow keeps hanging on.

We haven't started calving yet,
and though the wood pile's kind of low,
I'm holding off on cutting more,
until there ain't so darn much snow!

There, I've stacked up my excuses,
for avoiding other things that I should do,
instead of sitting here in the kitchen
trying to craft a rhyme or two.

The hardest part of being a poet,
is just to keep the guilt at bay,
and accept the fact that
sometimes it's my job,
to sit and think all day!

The Gathering

What ever happened to chasing cows,
and riding on the range?
The idea of a cowboy poetry gathering
might seem a little strange!

That cowboys might be thinking men,
who ponder some at night,
or ranch wives and lonely cowgirls,
would take the time to write,
in verse or prose their passing thoughts
on the happenings of the day,
or commit to rhyme the secret dreams,
they'd never dare to say.

Well of course there's cowboy poets!
The part that I find strange
is the way them city folks enjoy
our stories from the range!

Winter Across the Rockies

From Saskatchewan to
Texas the snow
is three feet deep,
gas bills are high, cow
feed is short,
and it buried all the sheep.

Good news all around
I'd say,
although it might be
brutal now.
There'll be moisture for
their crops come spring,
and green grass for a
cow.

The other thing about this weather turn,
that kind off makes me smile.
There's folks from Texas flying here,
to thaw out for a while!

Yes they are flocking here from near and far
from every corner of the west,
to praise their cows or mourn them sheep,
at the Kamloops Cowboy Fest!

Cow Country Christmas Memory

The cattle and horses got fed first,
That was a tradition at our place.
Christmas in cow country,
without that hectic urban pace.

Each of our ponies got an apple,
with their morning feed of oats,
as we hurried through our morning chores,
in felt pack boots and overcoats.

Mom served homemade eggnog,
Dad passed the presents out.
He did it slow to torment us,
of that I have no doubt.

From the Christmas of my childhood,
many memories linger on,
like snowy mittens, fresh sliced apples,
feeding cattle before dawn.

Pop always insisted that presents wait,
until the stock had all been fed.
He was sure surprised first time we had it done,
before he got out of bed!

The Christmas Tree Hunt

I'm a little out of breath from the climb,
this ol' cowboy was never real fond of walking.
We pour a little hot chocolate from the thermos,
and stare down at the valley without talking.

I remember two boys pulling a toboggan
up the long hill behind the house.
The trail wound through the sage along the rim of the draw
that led from the valley floor to the bench lands above.

The snow getting progressively deeper,
we climb straight up for an hour, on this labor of love.
My little brother and I, the youngest of five,
the ones left at home,
to keep the tradition alive.

The ponderosa pine in the creek draw below,
give way to the fir as higher we go.
We break over the top,
now in snow past our knees,
following the draw
passing judgment on trees.

As the sun gets some height,
the mist burns off below,
and the whole valley sparkles,
beneath its shroud of fresh snow.
We gaze down a while, it's an incredible view,
but to jaded young eyes, "Heck it ain't nothin' new!"

I guess I would have been twelve years old
(little brother was younger of course)
and our Christmas tree hunting was all done on foot,
because the trail was too slick for a horse.
We head on up the trail to the thicket we know,
where the draw peters out and the Christmas trees grow.

My daughter is laughing,
"Dad quit your day dreaming
we've still got to find a good tree."
It's three dozen years later, on the same rim of the valley,
and she's way more fussy than either little brother or me.

Adios Aught–3!

The past year was a rank one,
with lots of twists and turns,
the kind that leaves the best of hands,
with bruises and rope burns.

Now the boss has run a new one in,
that's bound to test our sand.
She'll pick up, where aught–3 left off,
so we'd better make our stand.

Snub'er up real quick,
and cinch your saddle tight.
If we get by the first few months,
she should turn out all right.

Old aught – 3 was a renegade,
who got a lot of good hands throwed.
I think this year will end up fair and gentle,
Once we get them first months rode!

Just Keep Dancin'!!!

Timing is the secret,
to a successful rain dance some will say.
I'll tell you here and now,
it just don't work that way.

Timing?
The decision?
When to start?
only affects the length of time
you must dance with all your heart!

Persistence, that's what really matters.
You must dance and beat the drum
for as long as takes
for your prayers to be heard,
and the rain to finally come!

Courage
For our friends and neighbors

The West
is creation's best,
sculpted by ice, wind, and fire.
Her children made to match the land,
twisted rawhide and barb wire.

The half moon hangs blood red,
over a valley choked with smoke.
Stillness beyond quiet,
no night bird or cricket sings
as nature waits in silent dread,
to see what tomorrow brings.

Have you heard the true voice of courage?
It's not the bravado of fighting men.
It's the whisper of a woman
standing in the ashes,
saying, "We shall build again!"

To All the Volunteers

Our valley is scorched bruised and battered,
but we all came out alive.
Giving thanks, for although so much was lost,
we managed to survive.

And from the ashes of the fire storm,
we have gleaned a wondrous treasure.
Diamonds of humanity,
forged by heat and pressure.

You fought beside us on the fire lines,
donated clothing, food, and cash,
brought hope and inspiration,
when our dreams had turned to ash.

Thank You!

Tales of the Cariboo Trail

It's been nearly two hundred years
since David Stuart rode up
from the South,
on a moccasin trail ten thousand
years old,
from the Okanagan River's mouth.

It was the trade route of the
Shuswap,
that would become the
Cariboo Trail.
Lifeline of British Columbia
before the coming of the rail.

The fur brigades and cattle drives,
the miners in search of gold,
followed the winding valley paths,
as did the human beings of old.

From Kamloops to the Columbia,
before the coming of the rails,
it was the lifeline of British Columbia,
and that road has many tales.

Royal Memories

As the Queen and Prince Philip
made their flying tour out West,
I wonder if the Duke recalled
when he'd been Chunky Woodward's guest.

In May and June of sixty-two,
he played cowboy for a while,
riding Chunky's quarter horses,
and learning the western style.

He grew quite fond of them I'm told,
and as the tales I've heard recount,
that a filly from the Douglas Lake,
later became his polo mount.

It's said that horses liked him too,
like the fancy dapple gray
that carried him with grace and style
throughout His Highness's stay.

The same gray that bucked Dave Batty off,
young Dave was stunned and embarrassed by this farce,
until Jimmy McDonnel pointed out,
"I guess you haven't got a royal arse!"

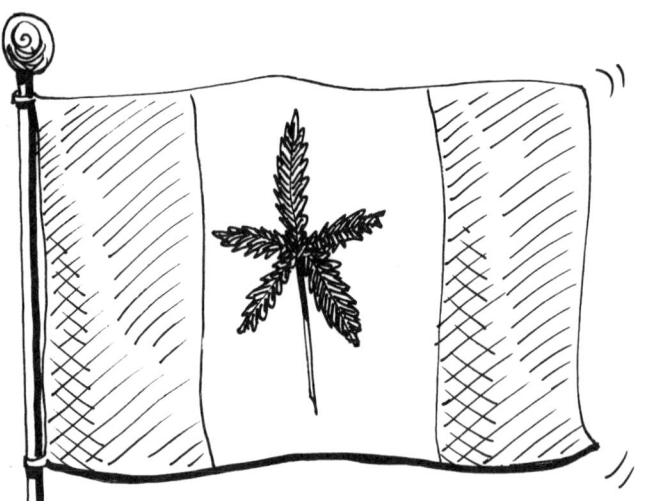

Like Wow Man!

In September 2002 the Canadian senate put their wise grey heads together and sent a message to Parliament suggesting they legalize marijuana. It has taken them quite a while but I think all them old hippies who sneaked north across the Medicine Line during the Vietnam War have pretty much taken over.

Well they've finally gone and done it,
this time there ain't no jokin'.
We'll never have to ask again,
what them old senators have been smoking.

So Jean Chretien can sign that Kyoto Accord,
but it won't make our air more clear,
when every pothead in the USA,
decides to move up here!

Like the Prohibition Days,
it will be boom times for a while,
as we all farm the wildwood weed,
and live it up in style!

But before them old hippies in the senate,
get to messin' with the law,
they best check with George
so we don't end up
like another Panama!

62

Weaning Time

I hauled the bay mare up to my brother's place,
and left the foal behind.
Having her momma out of calling range
sure speeds up the weaning time.

The mother cows are bawling
as we sort off the heifers and the steers.
Them cows can make at lot of noise,
but they never shed no tears.

We sure can't afford to keep them,
so the calves all have to go,
and the bawling seems more mournful,
than it did a year ago.

The little sorrel filly has settled in at home.
Born to be a cow horse, soon over the hills we'll roam.

She's fast, just like her momma, there's a promise in her stride.
So I have to cowboy up for a few more years,
I've got one more good horse to ride!

More western rhymes and songs from
HANCOCK HOUSE PUBLISHERS

Rhymes on the Range
Mike Puhallo, Brian Erannon,
Wendy Liddle
0-88839-368-7
5½ x 8½, sc, 64 pages

Meadow Muffins
Mike Puhallo, Wendy Liddle
0-88839-436-5
5½ x 8½, sc, 64 pages

Piled Higher and Deeper on the Cariboo Trail
Mike Puhallo, Wendy Liddle
0-88839-487-X
5½ x 8½, sc, 64 pages

Bards in the Saddle
Alberta Cowboy Poetry Society
0-88839-407-1
5½ x 8½, sc, 96 pages

Russell Country
Bette Wolf Duncan
0-88839-481-0
5½ x 8½, sc, 96 pages

Songs of the Pacific Northwest
Phil Thomas, Jon Bartlett, Ed.
0-88839-610-4
8½ x 11, sc, 208 pages

Rhymes of the Raven Lady
P.J. Johnson
0-88839-366-0
5½ x 8½, sc, 64 pages

The Best of Chief Dan George
Chief Dan George, Helmut Hirnschall
0-88839-544-2
5½ x 8½, sc, 128 pages

The Best of Robert Service
Robert Service, Mariken Van Nimwegen
0-88839-545-0
5½ x 8½, sc, 128 pages

View all HANCOCK HOUSE titles at **www.hancockhouse.com**